Software Industry Compatible Projects: For The New Engineer

Dr. Varun Gupta
Amity University, Noida

(Formerly with *National Institute of Technology, Hamirpur*, *PEC University of Technology, Chandigarh*, *Indian Institute of Technology, Mandi*)

Software Industry Compatible Projects: For The New Engineer
Varun Gupta

Printed and published by:

CreateSpace Independent Publishing Platform (An Amazon Company)

ISBN-13: 978-1978317147

ISBN-10: 197831714X

To my Parents, Sister and Aarit Gupta (My Nephew)

Acknowledgement

I take this opportunity to acknowledge the efforts of ocean of people that had close association with me in my life, with me playing a role of a child, student and a teacher. First I am thankful to my parents for bringing me to this level where I can see this world with the aptitude that gives me worth differentiable position than others.

I am grateful to Dr. Chetna Gupta and Dr. Maneesha who had not only worked hard on me during my studies but also continuously guiding me thereafter.

I am very thankful to Prof. Durg Singh Chauhan and Dr. (Mrs.) Kamlesh Dutta who taken a responsibility to give me an enriching experience of undertaking a research in Software Engineering. The research understanding and confidence gained after getting good research results followed by the strength gained after few failures, makes a person universal to quickly formulate and apply the research methodology wherever seen a problem, thereby contributing to the society.

I thank Prof. R.L Sharma who made me think about the real strength that was lying hidden inside me. Working with him was like an enriching experience for me in my life.

I firmly believe that the person is always guided by many great personalities that give turning points for bringing success in life. Such a great personality's, works on "give" relationship thereby making the "take" as unnecessary. Understanding the hidden strength and employing it for society is the activity that was carved out due to the continuous support, trust and continuous advice of above special persons that I met in my life.

Preface

The project development is the primary requirement for better and long lasting understanding of the theory. The students are not well exposed to complex project development during their engineering degree and in fact undertake small or some medium complexity project in their pre final or final year. The development of small projects are undertaken in less risky and less dynamic environment since many of the projects are not coordinated with the industries and are developed in small team size with faculty in charge as one of the stakeholder.

The development practices are in fact not completely based on those mentioned in literature and not on those followed in industries. Effort of any student is to just to submit some working version of the software and the underlying problem definition on the which the software is based, is not well positioned in terms of its applicability to industry or the society suffering from the problem.

The students are not well prepared to better employ the software engineering principles and not in position to do optimal selections of the development models as per project characteristics.

The engineering student should have the freedom to select his own area of expertise and therefore must work to gain specialization in it. Such knowledge will help him acquire higher education in concerned area.

Small projects may provide student sound skills of programming and will lead to better understanding of the theoretical subjects. Medium or large complexity projects in the chosen area will motivate student not only gain hands-on experiences on live project development in almost real simulated environment but also to employ his understandings of the computer science theory as gained though development of various small projects into bigger live project.

This book gives some guidelines of how to implement small, medium and large complexity live projects throughout the engineering degree. The book is motivated by the experiences of the author with the project development undertaken by students and hence may not be the representation of all students/institutions.

The information contained in this book is based on the experience of the author as a teacher and a researcher in India. Thus the information is like a guideline and the success rate may not be completely based on the contained guidelines as it depends on many factors like student attributes, industry openings (or recession) etc. Thus these guidelines are to be considered "Nice to Have/Follow".

These guidelines will surely motivate the student about need for continuously integrating new advanced layer of knowledge over the previous one and the need for exposure to practical skills. The author may not be taken responsible for any loss or happening with any one as a result of contained guidelines.

Chapter 1

INTRODUCTION

The software industry expects the engineering institutes and universities in general to produce industry compatible product with sound theoretical knowledge and highly practical skills. In normal bachelor in Technology curriculum the students undergo through theory subjects followed by laboratory exercises in order to gain practical understanding of the theory. Students are some time encouraged to do smaller projects and medium complexity projects in last year of engineering. One question makes us think that whether the students are really compatible enough to handle industrial live problems especially in their last year? It might be Ok for few, but according to me definitely not with all of the students. The straightforward reason is that few students had the experience of just handling class room small projects while remaining of them hardly had such a small project hands-on.

Lack of familiarity of employing the software development process in industries might be a limiting factor in handling industrial problems.

Stating in other words, the lack of practical knowledge of implementing the small challenging development tasks or lack of understanding of the appropriate development methodology like Agile, the experience or the knowledge that can be glued together is missing as the prerequisite experience for undertaking the industrial live problems. For example, even if the student knows well the concepts of programming language like C, concept of data structure, concept of file handling and had implemented a small class projects using these concepts, but rarely know the use of software development methodology then the net output in the development of any complex project will be non deterministic. This is because the student is unaware of handling the practical realities of development like dynamism in user requirements, stakeholders, experience in handling stakeholders etc. In case of lack of knowledge in implementing small projects, the practical knowledge of theoretical knowledge might be limited and the situation will be very bad for such a student.

Thus the student must understand the importance of supplementing the knowledge he acquires during his degree with the project development at different stages of varying complexities. The projects must be developed using appropriate methodology so that the student faces the development challenges very early and thus handling industrial projects becomes enriching experience for him.

With every software industry working in a competitive market, efforts are to convince the stakeholders and clients by delivering the best quality product that has a competitive edge. A student with the degree in any engineering branch is eligible to work in the software industry due to various roles required to be played by the company employees. The software industry requires candidates of different areas of interest, different expertise, and different experience, but with a high degree of self motivation. For example, a company producing a mass market product may require software engineers that are required to work as analysts, designers, database experts, programmers (like mobile app developers, web developers, etc.), Domain experts, testers and persons with good management skills to look the overall management of development process especially agile projects.

Thus, for every engineering student, whether interested in artificial intelligence, networking, software engineering, programming etc., has a role to play in the software industry. A person with an interest in artificial intelligence may be required to work as domain expert and may contribute to the overall development of software for artificial intelligence projects. So the interest of computer students or students of other branches does not come in the path of their selection in the software industry due to the demand of people of different expertise and capabilities. Now the question that

4

comes in one mind related to:

- Student capabilities i.e. since software industry is interested in a person that can take multiple roles, so what artefacts are to be targeted by students to maximize their selections?

- What strategy the students should follow for the development of projects as per their interests during their engineering?

The first question is difficult to answer with full confidence due to different and dynamic needs of industry and continuously growing Information Technology. The students must have theoretical as well as practical knowledge. Since the theoretical and practical knowledge will incorporate many subjects thus undergoing trough all of them in limited period of 4 years will be very tedious, tiring as well as boring for few of students. To make situation somewhat easy for students, I recommend students to gain mastery in few programming languages, back ends and software engineering.

Depending on the student interest, gained knowledge can be utilized to master subjects like networking, distributed databases protocols etc. Since the Information Technology is too vast, industry demands many roles and students have different expectations & experiences (some students start programming in schools) thus this question is not very easier to answer. This question can only be answered as per experiences of a person.

It is accepted that the project development encourages students to apply their theoretical knowledge into practice and this process may allow them to learn new things. New learning is attributable to the use of programming constructs in a meaningful manner and in fact, it becomes highly encouraging for them to understand user requirements, draw DFD and transform it into working models. During development of medium or large complexity projects, the students not only employ the expertise of the development of small projects, but also will try using different tools so as

6

to minimize effort and time. Students may also try employing reusability to get good quality product at earliest since the student will be pressurized for quick delivery of the software in the form of near evaluations or ending academic semester. Once the students have completely designed software, and let's assume it is working fine. The student will be highly motivated and full of confidence to show the running code to project in change. Some changes proposed will make students think about the fact that why things gone wrong and where the mistakes were made. This will add to his experience and will be reflected in the quality of software development of any new project or later increments. The student will also learn the manner of handling dynamism in form of implementing the unexpected changes required by the user, provided that good feedback is given by project in a charge / team. The presence of such feed backs will help students working in mass market developments.

Thus, if the student has the opportunity to develop

some project for the duration of a degree or different projects during his degree then this will involve lots of learning. In fact the student may be well adapted to work on live industrial problems in the last year of his degree.

To produce industry competent candidates, the institutes must make the project development mandatory as a separate course or as a mandatory evaluation of theory course or laboratory sessions.

To be able to work on live problems, students must have exposure to many small and medium complexity projects. The distinct university curriculum should not come as a hindrance in providing sound project development practice to students.

Chapter 2

PROJECT DEVELOPMENT DURING B.TECH DEGREE

The below mentioned guidelines could be a wise strategy for the students to supplement the engineering education with project developments. The faculty should give students a brief understanding of software development models so that they could have hands-on each model during their engineering course. The model to be introduced depends on the complexity of the project that student is handling (i.e. the academic year of the course). For first two years he can use models like waterfall, spiral etc while in third year student should develop skills to use and implement agile models.

- During the first year, the student must implement small projects using C language. In universities offering C and

C++ together, it's better to do using C if the student has new to the language. Otherwise, if the student has done basic C previously, then the project in C using advanced concepts or new project in C++ can be undertaken. For such a student, some previously implemented project can be identified for being transformed into C++ code. Such a previous project may be one that implemented some advanced topics like graphics, hash tables etc, so as to strengthen not only C++ skills but also advanced topic knowledge of the student.

- During the second year, students should be asked to transform the previous C software project into C++ so that they may get the picture of transition from non object oriented language to object based. The effort saved in implementing the new project in above mentioned manner rather than implementing from scratch, should be employed implemented the above C++

project using all data structures so as to bring visibility about how the data structure selection may improve the working efficiency of the program. Other advanced concepts like graphics, file structures etc can be added subjected to the condition that the topics are well discussed as a part of the theory or extra hours. In case, the student has already implemented advanced level projects in the previous year, then he must work, adding more advanced features, working on optimizations etc. Hands on experiences on file handling, may prove to be a future road map for database management system.

• During the third year, the student must get expertise about web development and database development. At this stage, student after implementing few web pages in class or laboratory should either

11

transform their C++ projects into web project or should implement new one from the scratch. Since the student require to know Hypertext markup language (HTML), tools like Dreamweaver, elementary client side scripting language like Javascript, VB script and server side scripting language like ASP or PHP, so the whole process can be decomposed into two semesters:

- o Semester 1: Working on static part and client side scripting.
- o Semester 2: Working on server side scripting and integrating with static part & databases. The databases can be implemented in either semester depending on the semester in which databases are taught.

Students may also be very interested in third year in projects related to AI,

Networking, Software Engineering etc which may require them to learn new languages (like LISP for AI) or just require new problem statement (the new domain system is to be developed) alone. Former case puts more challenges on students since they need to learn a new language and get practical skills. The whole semester academics are to be adjusted accordingly. So it's better for these students to consider this as a self learning exercise and do the project development at the end of the third semester. Later case requires students to gain some insights into practical's of the new domain like network programming, which not only requires knowledge of languages like C but knowledge of concepts like creating sockets, creating connections etc. Finalizing the problem statement will require students to do some small practical's and then in consultation

13

with faculty in charge may decide the suitable project.

Further, it is better that student can analyze and document the experiences of employing the different development models till third year as the term paper or small project. Such a document will be quite helpful to him in the final year when he has a different complexity problem to solve, different resources and varying level of expertise, which may guide him selecting and using an appropriate development model. This term paper is required because there exists many software development models whose employability is different for different projects with varying complexities, timelines, categories, resources available and expertise of developers.

- During the final year, It's now the turn to employ the knowledge and skills acquired in previous years to handle industrial live problems. Students can go for two types of projects:

o   Industrial live problems (IP).
o   Live research problems (RP).

Although live research problems are similar to live industrial problems since every research problem needs to be validated in industrial settings, but the difference lies in the fact that industrial project problems are the problems/expectations that are given to industries by their clients. Such expectations are the description of the new software to be developed or the problems as faced in the client organizations. Industry may give student partial or complete problems statement depending on the number of students working as a team, their expertise and so on. Such a team will have many experts of the industry as its senior members and student may have many things to learn and contribute. The industrial live problems may not demand automation and may represent the need for generating solutions to the problems as faced in the area or client organization. For example, a client may give a problem statement that he wants to automate tax generation & collection process. He may ask the organization to analyze the problems of low revenues as the client had expected high tax but reverse happened. In such situation industry may involve student to first analyze the situation, do some research and generate a solution. If the problem is due to some black money like issues, he may suggest client getting tax generation & collection to be done through automatic ways. Thus, industrial live problems in general may or may not end with automation. When we talk about the software industry, live problems may represent the new software requirements or may represent problems as faced during software development process. In the latter case, to better reduce time and effort in carrying out the required development process, the automation of the elicited problem solution will be the best option.

Research problems are the problems that are elicited from doing a systematic literature survey and hence represent the various problems for which the research community aims to find the most suitable answer. The problem statement as elicited after analysis of literature is the result of gathering papers related to the survey and critical analysis of the gathered papers. The solution of such a problem may provide industry relief and thus may be most suitable for their practices.

Engineering students can derive the problem statement himself, the solution to the derived problem and finally the automation tool as the product. Otherwise, he may automate the solution given by any other researcher followed by proper citation in the project report. In such case, the student just needs to analyze the importance of the area and hence the work by getting input from industry and then must proceed to get the automation done. Some universities may allow the submission of research problem, solution and validation results as the engineering project, but most likely such projects are submitted as executable softwares. For example, in software engineering, the software industry may be impacted with the elicited problem and may want not only a solution to the problem, but also its automation to save time and effort in carrying out the activity. Many research works as disseminated in the research papers end with after validation of proposal on live data set and hence such works can be a boom for the student in providing automation support. The research problem aims to provide validated solutions to the problems as faced in the concerned area and thus may or may not attract attention for automation. However, we expect student to end with automated processes.

For both the two types of projects, the student works in his own area of interest (like software engineering, Networking, AI etc) for which he has gained different experiences of small projects with the ability to learn new things including languages. Some students might prefer the problems (industrial and research) that start with some research & may or may not prefer ending with automation while some may prefer those that start with the automation. Such projects boost up practical skills, theoretical knowledge and research aptitude.

In the software industry, it normally happens that the software engineer is given the task that he had never done before like new module to be developed in a new language in just a night. It is his experience of previous (although unrelated projects) and confidence level of software engineer. With the increased number of projects developed by the student, the confidence and experience increases.

An advantage of the research problem and research based industrial live problems are that the student gains research experience and develop skills performing critical analysis of other researchers works. The student interacts with industry to validate research problems and thus better positions itself to defend the research proposal. Once the defense is made, the student is in a right advantageous position to start working on the problem and implement the validated solution. This generates the sense of responsibility among them.

The details about implementing research based project are given in Chapter 3.

Chapter 3
IMPLEMENTING RESEARCH BASED PROJECTS

The researchers work in different areas of the domain. In each domain, the researchers target specific problems, analysis of these problems and proposed solutions may help other researcher's present critique of the available solutions thereby leading to the identification of research gaps. The identification of limitations in the available techniques (literature in general) and identification of unexplored areas may motivate the researcher to work on these areas and suggest mechanisms to improve them. The improvements may be automated to further reduce time and effort to carry out an activity. For example, in the area of software engineering, researcher may automate the regression testing activity by automating some well known regression testing technique or his own

proposed and validated techniques. Thus the
researcher can automate either of the two research
problems:

- The problems of other researchers whose
  solutions are already identified and
  evaluated
- New problems identified by researcher for
  which he has proposed and evaluated the
  solution. Such a method is suitable if a
  student has large time at his disposal
  typically a year, with finding of research
  presented as minor project and tool as a
  major project. The publication of the
  project details as the paper or as the patent
  will be a plus point.

Irrespective of the mechanism used/method used for
automation, the steps to do a research based project
remains the same. The strategy to implement the
research based projects includes the following:

1. The student should identify the area of interest. If he is interested in software engineering then he must choose the sub areas like Requirement Engineering, design, testing etc. Such sub areas can be further decomposed at lower, but a finer level like model driven testing, model driven architecture etc. If he is interested in two different areas like Intrusion detection and software engineering, then such type of interdisciplinary research and project development can be facilitated in doing below mentioned steps of a literature survey and analysis on these two areas separately. Finally, the outcome of the two areas must be analyzed together to fetch out meaningful problems. The selection may be based on the interests of the students and/or his prior knowledge about the area. The inputs from industry, expert advice and faculty guidelines will be very beneficial to the student. Below mentioned activities are to

be performed to identify areas of sub area at the proper level of abstraction.

a) Search the best bibliographic databases to analyze the sub areas targeted by other researchers. Since the amount of knowledge gap of student might be large enough and he may not be able to cover it up if duration of research is smaller say 2 months. So if the duration is smaller, researcher may try getting inputs from project in charge, other researchers and industry about the area that is lacking sound techniques and automation. Thus the selection of sub area for the smaller duration project can be facilitated with inputs from various sources like faculty, researchers and industry.

If the duration is larger, he may try reading a few papers and may try getting ideas about how things are going on in the area. Again the inputs from various sources are required.

The net outcome is that the researcher has analyzed the sub area and same areas might feel more exciting than others. Few areas might be seen of more potential while some may not by industry people. The excitement of a student about a particular area is attributable to the less knowledge gap, student interest's match, familiarity with the area etc.

In case, nothing meaningful is extracted, it is advised to target any known area the student has studied in his theory.

b) Once he has selected area, student might have some "foggy" picture of the selected area. At this stage, industry inputs can be obtained to let industry see the potential of the area. Since the selection of the project will determine its deadline and no deadline is to be skipped in academics, industry might select the area on the basis of expertise of the student, his knowledge, effort and time he had to spend on the project. The selected sub area will then be analyzed for problems it is facing; solutions will be generated and finally automating thereby benefitting the industry.

2. Once the sub area is selected, the student needs to identify the problem so that the solution can be prepared, evaluated and automated. The selection of the sub area might make students aware of different proposed solutions and he may be in a position to better analyze the solution or select the best one. The selection of better solution gives him the option to automate the solution provided that the selected solution be well recognized, well appreciated by other researchers and well evaluated thereby having a strong tendency

to bring improvement in the area. Automation of the above technique will further improve the area targeted.

The selection of the available solution for automation involves the following:

a) Read latest papers (maximum upto past 5 years).

b) Analyze the article metrics like citations, author comments etc.

c) Try to categorize the survey papers depending on the problem targeted, working algorithm, and datasets used etc.

d) Analyze the papers of each category and select the highest potential paper of each category.

e) Compare the above selected high potential paper depending on:

- Impact.
- Student Interest.
- Industry feedback.

- Student resources.
- Feasibility etc.

f) Select the highest potential paper.

g) Read the selected highest potential papers. Stress on the working algorithm, results and execution of the algorithm (if available else execute the algorithm on your sample project/dataset) to get a clean picture of the paper.

3. Select the software development methodology. I recommend trying to understand and employ the development methodology as per applicable for your project. Such employability is decided on the basis of your finding of term paper on Software Engineering project submitted previous year.

a) Send the paper for reading to industry and project in charge so that they can express their expectations/requirement about the software that is automating the technique disseminated in the selected paper.

b) Send mail to the author of the above paper or other authors that are working in same/related areas for their advice/feedback. Also collect the software requirement submitted by them.

c) Incorporate the feedbacks obtained from different sources. Take union of the requirement obtained as per updated feedback set. The requirement set should be further refined to remove any missing requirements, ambiguities etc.

d) Sort the requirements into functional and non functional requirements.

e) Ask the industry participants to select most important requirements (both functional and non functional) so that the project can be completed within the deadline. In such projects the industry will be able to drop minimal functional requirements and maximum non functional requirements as one need to implement complete technique as disseminated in the research paper. In such cases, the industry may collaborate to undertake the development work of those requirements that are impossible to be developed by the student in academic deadlines and resources.

f) Develop the working system using the activities as defined in the employed software development model.

g) It's better to get the beta testing done in industrial settings. Slight modifications might be required in the final project.

h) Report of the software will be based on the available research extended by the student.

In case the student wants to propose a new problem statement in order to automate the proposed solution of the new problems, then the below mentioned steps are required to be followed:

a) Read latest papers (maximum upto past 5 years). Such papers are extracted on the basis of the query string against which you trigger the bibliographic databases. The query string formulation could be benefitted from the experience you have drawn in selection of sub area and feedback from industry and faculty.

b) Perform the critical analysis of the extracted papers. Such a critical analysis will make you think about the limitation of available research if related to some other aspect of the domain selected.

c) Critical analysis will help you frame problem statement at some degree of abstraction; still it will be too broad at this stage.

d) Narrow down the problem statement by getting input from industry and faculty.

e) Start working on solution generation- which could be a new technique or a survey based research. Since we are talking about automation, so this book considers that solution is in the form of new technique.

f) Employ the solution on live dataset and if results are promising then start automating the proposed technique. The appropriate software development model can be used.

Chapter 4

OVERALL OUTCOME

The guidelines as given in this book if followed by the student (Even flexibly) may give a credit of many projects of divine complexities and enriching experiences to the student. The student will have the opportunity to not only get familiar with the skills required to implement projects using appropriate development methodology but also to get the flavour of risky and uncertain software development process in industrial settings.

The student as buddy software engineer, will not only bother about the functionality, time and cost, but will also welcome the changes required in his delivered product with the right attitude.

The student will also be in a continuous process of always searching for better ways of doing the things thereby replacing the old code fragments with new highly efficient ones. This continuous work and research feeling will boost up knowledge and practical skills of the student. Further, he will be an asset for any mass market development firms owing to continuous delivery and improvements required in the process, which is facilitated with the continuous working aptitude of the student. Such a student will be ideal for both research centres and development centres of the software industry.